Words to Touch

Unlikely words from bars

LEON G. WOODS

WestBow Press books may be ordered through booksellers or by contacting:

WestBow Press
A Division of Thomas Nelson & Zondervan
1663 Liberty Drive
Bloomington, IN 47403
www.westbowpress.com
844.714.3454

Interior Image Credit: Alexis C. Woods

ISBN: 978-1-6642-0496-6 (sc)
ISBN: 978-1-6642-0497-3 (e)

Library of Congress Control Number: 2020917156

Print information available on the last page.

WestBow Press rev. date: 10/12/2020

WESTBOW
PRESS®
A DIVISION OF THOMAS NELSON
& ZONDERVAN

Words to Touch

John, Raymond, Terry

3-9-14

Three amigos, three men who are my friends.

Three dads, three husbands who could not pretend the end.

Three souls, three lives that some would say are gone too soon.

Thinking of them brings to heart the part we shared in life.

All three forever live: our God forgives; His Son lives.

Twenty-Five Years

7-5-11 7:02 p.m.

It began on this day,

a day to behold our love told before Him.

Our family and friends attended the vows said before Him.

A day of food and fun—we danced; we drank and thought of life to come with Him at the head.

Sixteen

11-21-10 & 12-7-10 4:03 p.m.

Today is her day;

she is special. Say hey for this day; thank God in every way.

Sixteen years ago small, today tall.

A big smile that lights a mile.

Dark eyes that pierce

but not always fierce.

Determined and strong, decidedly true.

A Love Down Deep for My Brothers and My Sisters

11/19/04

Sometimes it's said; sometimes it's read. Other times, it's in prayer.

The perfect love of Christ is the model.

The example is His life on earth.

Giants

10-28-11

Little did we know the large character of them. They would drink straight whiskey with a chase of ice water as they played cards. The laughter was loud. Proud was the laughter as we listened not from afar. Sometimes, we were allowed to take part in the cards. Bid whisk was the game. Always lots of talk, back and forth, good-natured fun that entertained everyone.

They smoked because of the time period. Filterless squares were the flavor. The drink and smoke were strong, for they were strong; they savored life. They worked hard and enjoyed time together even harder. Their lives contained constant improvement for all who came into the family. The family was large, extended, and immediate. Extended family meant longtime friends, often from childhood. Immediate family was uncles, aunts, cousins, brothers, sisters, parents, grandparents, and all the offspring.

They believed in the one and only God. Their faith grew as they moved away from the world and its false promises. Jesus was the model they chose to emulate. They taught the thought of freedom from hate. Love not hate was what they would imitate for Jesus's sake.

I watched from afar as they reached for the star—the star of Jesus and the galaxy of God's promises. How little did I know what I was seeing and what I would come to believe. The bar was set high, how high; today, I know the reason why.

A spiritual life, a principled life was their code. Family was everything, not just a mode of thought. They taught without thought about their part. The talk matched the walk. I now know I learned from giants of life, of love, of spiritual gifts. There was no rift, no anger, no selfishness, only love to lift us on their shoulders.

Their spirits are still large; they live in part in our hearts. The lessons learned burn hot today, for it is now our turn to talk and walk. Remember the giants; remember the shoulders that make us stand tall above the world and its judgments. Remember the giants: God In Action, Never Taught Selfishness.

Giants are among us; they live and teach by example of spiritual unconditional love.

Wife's Bible

3/23/05

A book of verse, a look at someone who is sometimes a nurse.

Sometimes a New Testament is carried in their purse.

The whole Bible always comes to church.

My wife's Bible reminds me of the Christian life she leads.

Reminds me of life that God has placed in us.

My wife's Bible brings to mind

spiritual growth we have shared.

The verse on the cover reflects her true self and thoughts of who God is to her.

My wife's Bible is full of Christ's love for the church and us.

The Bible is full of love, and so is my wife.

Fiftieth Birthday

6/18/05

The day you created me, I was small in all ways but loved by you.

I can never grow out of my dependence on you.

I pray for you to continue to nurture me.

I pray to always stay away from the pride that divides me from you.

Small and obedient, your nourishment is what the need be.

A Husband's Wait

3/29/05

While she shops,

I sit and think about why I am here.

It is clear:

to spend time doing what she likes.

To offer a yes or no.

To wait and grow in patience,

to enjoy the gift of marriage.

God made us one,

so when she shops, we shop.

God's Gifts, My Children

8/3/02

My children I give thanks for every day.

God has loaned them to me.

I must teach, love, and care for them from my heart.

I should not hold back any part of my heart for them.

Thank you, God, for their love and life.

May I draw closer to you to bring them always in your presence.

Dear God, may I, may we do the job well.

It would be so swell to see them as adults loving you, Jesus, and the Holy Spirit.

May you (God) always be a period and not a question mark in our lives.

Mine, Yours, Ours

1/18/1996

Ownership of precious things, two of same mind can do anything.

A wellspring of human thought

often brings about a oneness between different offspring.

Genetics don't mean a thing when we speak of precious beings.

Under God's influence,

we become merely human beings.

Girl with Teeth and Pretty Smile

4/18/1996

Title by Rhonda L. Terry
Prose by Leon G. Woods

Tiny face full of grace.

Eyes clear that know no fear.

Hair that's fine but oh, so fair.

Teeth of white

didn't come to be overnight.

A smile that lights the room

like flowers in bloom.

Unexpected Riches

6/21/1996

A baby was born today in a normal way.

Her parents expected a male; God made her female.

Instantly, a name appeared;

much to our delight, it sounds very right.

It flows, it has rhythm, everyone agreed it was to be.

So small in size,

but she is the ultimate prize in our eyes.

We are rich because of God's unexpected gift.

Baby Girl

1/1/1995

In the world, precious in my sight.

A sight of God's might.

My heart takes flight.

God's right and might will keep us trying with all our might

no matter what the plight.

A long time in coming

but always right on time.

Thank you, God, for allowing us to fight

for this precious sight.

Your hand of hands has been all the light.

Diamonds in the Rough

10/16/03

They weren't produced overnight,

but here they are, shining bright.

A light to see, though

they be unnoticed by some.

The sum of their worth

is not of this earth.

Who are we to say

what a diamond is, anyway?

Uncut they sometimes are,

but a diamond in the rough

will be cut to shape

and shined to brilliance by God's design.

20

Blood

4/30/1993

To see the blood of my blood spilled.

To see the blood is no thrill.

Understand the needless waste of time and space.

The blood is etched in time.

That blood lost is committed

to my mind.

The blood of my blood is not stopped,

for it is a special blood kind.

Family

6/3/1993

Conversation, aggravation, upsets, and hedging bets all lead to things of no consequence.

Women caring for, leaning on, confiding in each other

is like no other earthly situation.

Feelings of closeness thought out, often not talked about.

The atmosphere can be seen by any that this between the many is true; it could never be misconstrued.

Good and bad twice the love of many is

unmoving, consistent; and faithful; no never is

it hateful. Often it is said we don't care by the many, but if it were, no person would know.

Only the many know because it is unseen;

no kind of light or dark can hold it back.

The spirit that exists is of a strange twist. Harboring resentment is bewilderment. This unseen thing is like a rock wall; it will last for generations.

It resides in our hearts; besides, it's unseen,

mostly by the meaning love untold.

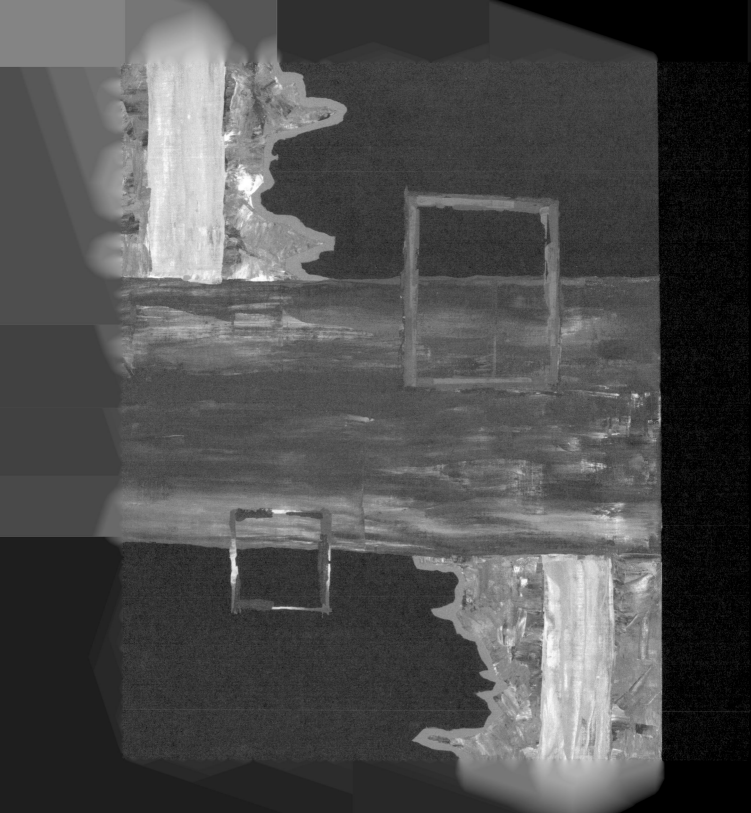

Mother's Day

5/9/1993

My thoughts are good lasting impressions,

like an oil painting.

My heart is good.

Scars are healing,

healing from my selfishness.

My mother is in final resting.

Her teachings are with me, guiding me still.

My mother taught life,

not hatefulness and self-will.

Mothers are more than special,

for their lives bring more life—and with more life, chance of a world involved in no strife.

California Cowboy

5/9/1993

Traveling by truck, carrying the load.

Bricks and mortar, sweat and love.

A belief in the unseen coming from above.

Doing what's said, the words are a bond.

Tying us together, knowing only family abounds.

Mountains and snow—

beauty beyond imagination.

Air and water clear and clean.

Gambling is a pastime within reasonable means.

Fought and worked for this nation.

Gave a lot without objection.

True to all, no separation.

Brother Blue

9/16/05

Brother, I miss you!

I miss your words of wisdom.

I miss your smile.

I miss the clear path your words gave to me.

We fought;

you taught me a way of life.

You always were about love.

You made sense of things often wondered about.

The why, we don't know the questions to ask for the answers of God's meaning in our lives.

I miss you, brother blue.

You are still true blue.

My Sister Rahab

3/17/08

It's that time,

the time when angels define

the divine what, where, and how. Angel of what?

Where angels are found.

How angels come to be for you and me.

Look past outward appearance;

look for the beauty of a soul discerned.

Whatever happened

brought you to a life of peace through hardship.

I smile awhile.

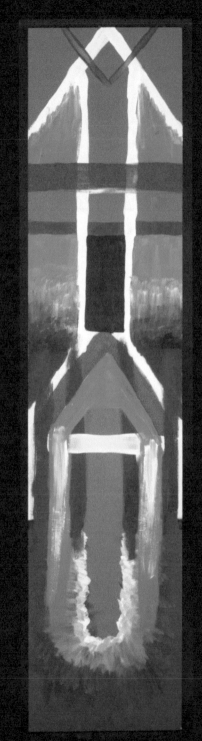

Cleaning Greens

11/18/07

I think of things,

the learning how and why from watching.

The gratitude of and for the person who taught.

Thankful for the mind that remembers

and those who will partake of the clean greens.

I appreciate more and more with each passing year what was learned by eye.

May I try to be a person whom others learn from by the eye.

Shoe Store Nordstrom

11/24/07

Giving thanks for things

that are not in a money bank.

Giving thanks for not falling

for Satan's pranks.

Giving thanks for the family ranks

and their love that fills up a most special bank.

Thanks for placing family

high on both our thanks.

A Sunday at Home

7/1/07

Not on purpose,

but forgot my keys.

I did pray on knees.

I felt a need to be there,

a need to be with Thee.

What a strange thing to be at home

when church is where I should be.

As I Wait

1/28/09

The mistake I make takes shape on the heart.

The part of life defined in mind by faith.

I try to imitate Him,

so I think of His life in me.

I wait for this life to take shape.

Faking is not the intent;

every moment of the day,

I should take thought of mankind's mistake.

I wait for the day when it is clear

He is here—no mistake, no fear.

I hear the voice, small but proud, because He speaks to a crowd.

A crowd filled with faith

as He takes place royally

among the human race.

Are You Trying to Save Souls or Just Those That Are Dressed Up?

Title: Ken Scott
2015
Prose: Leon G. Woods

Cover, covering, coverage of the

body, mind, and spirit.

The body and mind will decay.

Spirit stays even though

mostly unseen by human means, sight and touch.

Old days covered with our best to meet, greet, and share faith. Past and present teachings bring

God your best. Your first fruits might be the main idea.

A fashion show is nice, but is this a cover

of what they are thankful for or to hide a not-so-pleasant side?

Times past, our best was a freshly washed, starched, and pressed skirt, dress, shirt, and coveralls. Today, it might not be a suit but a nice pair of pants, shirt, or nice jeans.

No matter, it will be clean and seen as the

best of things we have to bring. Our quest to

bring our best or dress up our best should be

less about an outward show.

The main feature is showing up with best-dressed heart, mind, and soul, plus knowing God's in control. Was Jesus a clotheshorse or nicely robed for the mission, ministry, and heavenly goal?

Family

7/12/15

We gather to celebrate

what we are about.

We consider each other's goodness.

The things held dear are made clear.

We love, we talk, we play, we cook,

we hug, we shop, we drop the world talk.

Leaning on each other's strengths and

weaknesses, we gain no fame or shame.

Service is our leaderboard.

Board games, card games, not

gamesmanship is our intent. Pure joy

of being family is our remedy.

We run interference for pain to not be claimed.

The aim is a quiet faith to replace the loss. Our love is a loud statement said without

words.

A Friend of Friends

1/26/13

A dinner, some food, a lot of talk,

not much to feel out. Conversation flows, getting to know a new friend.

From beginning to end, comfortable, supportable friends.

Old and new in plain view, nothing to hide, no taking sides. Family situation similar,

some peculiar things but true for all

made room to not be misused.

Getting on with life, doing well when all is said. Friendship is easy when the new becomes old. All is told; no one is cold.

Hold on to what is true.

Learn from the new, combined with the old,

more love to behold.

Emmaus Walk

9/27/02

In our high-tech age,

I watch the men of praise. These men raise praise to the Trinity.

I watch the unpacking of high-tech tools.

The tools are used to school us in our walk

and talk that life is all about Jesus.

We seek to understand what more of the light will be revealed.

May we not be fence riders or deniers.

We seek to be sealed; we speak to be healed.

Our walk is not for recognition

or for first or second position.

The walk we talk is all about our Lord

and His word.

Morning Chaos

9/26/05

Wake the kids after I get off my knees.

Turn on the morning news.

Make some coffee to aid the wakeup process.

Get out of the shower, dress, and brush.

Drop one off at crossing station. Drop the other at school.

Back home to prepare for the ortho appointment. Get the dog out, feed and water. Take a break to pray, pray for the day. Make it to the ortho appointment.

Another couple cups of coffee.

Feeling at ease, the people are nice.

The conversation is real between me and the doc. Now on the way to school, then on to work.

OG Giant

We once called them the old people. We called them old-fashioned. All they were were giants. The truth was clear; their words we hold dear. The world was slower by today's standards. So, we thought of them as slow. The same as our young do us today.

They blazed trails that we stand on today. They fought the spiritual battle of good over evil, right over wrong. They fought to vote; the quotes were not jokes. The marches took courage beyond belief, for physical fighting was not a release. The songs that were sung contained social and political content. Old spirituals were sung to keep spirits high. Gospel songs and Bible verses fed the hunger of better days ahead.

Everyone was a brother; everyone was a sister. Camaraderie was a rule; every person had a place in the struggle. Not one was unimportant. The pain was shared; the strain of the load foretold many lifted together. In the store, in the church, on the bus, they had a resolve to better themselves and their offspring. They bore a spiritual ethic that invaded to the core. The faith was not porous. It was rock at the core.

We would listen to learn, and later in our lives, learned that what we were being taught was how to win in life. They might not have lived in ivory towers. They were not corporate giants. They were not bankers, doctors, lawyers, or industry leaders, but they were great family leaders. They were giants of the faith. They were of honesty and heart. Integrity was a brother; respect was clear and worth more than gold.

The dress was always the best, for their culture passed the test. Culture was clear; they had set the trend in invention, medicine, science, design of all kind.

Giants, giants, giants: God-Inspired, Anointed, Noteworthy, Truly Spiritual!

Thanksgiving 2014: Food and Family

Buy the hams for the family. Fire up the smokers.

Season the hams: that's the plan. Travel by land to the family land with the ham. Arrive safe because of God's grace. Greetings all around; the love abounds. Preparations are made as the food is made ready. Steady are the hands of the clan as we plan the deal of the meal.

Brine is the wine for the turkey. Adding ice makes the spice right. Sage plus green apples flavor the fowl. Season in, season out, it is about the love to be thankful to God, thankful for food. Thanks for the

feeding of body and soul while surrounded by God and family.

Potato and salad made a way to say that love went into the making. Gravy is smooth, not wavy.

Rice is made to accommodate the gravy. Yes, it's heavy, because the giblets, livers, and turkey necks add the weight. Turkey meat, light or dark, pays the freight of the sleep that awaits.

The Indians and Puritans years ago knew the score—to be thankful for the bounty before them. Great was the thanks; against the odds, they made the grade. High fashion was not offered; fancy food was not prepared. Plain and simple, the meal revealed. Modern day, it is still most often the same way. As Christians, we gather to celebrate what we've been graced to enjoy. The four *F*s at their best: food, family, friends, and faith.

Food prepared with love. The unconditional love from family. Extended hand of friendships old and new. Faith in the unseen being, but ever-present love, grace, and mercy from God. Every day in the hood of life, we should give Him thanks for His giving in every way.

Sometimes you think, *Okay, but it is not true according to who?* There are days when family is all. But they are not throwing you a ball. Many times, there is nothing you can say that defers the commonplace conversation. Friends and family show their love with much verbal jabbing and ribbing. The fun begins when the assumed is revealed.

Family comes in many ways: groups, extended, immediate, work, spiritual, church, cigar buddies, riding buddies, bloodline—so many ways and days we are blessed.

Fun assumptions, not gossip and corruptions, make plentiful the laughter. Fun assumptions provide an actor to appear that has no fear of life, and it is always nice to hear their lines read aloud.

Only family can tease and please the soul all at the same time. Only family knows you well enough to console and promote all at the same time. The mind is a wellspring of thoughts about what is good and right. The family often brings to light all with their might, illuminated rights.

My Sister

6/7/06

Full of love and grace,

sometimes love and hate, she certainly filled a place of mind. Her eyes never lied.

Dark and large were the windows to her soul. Tough but gentle were the heart and mind; oftentimes, she lived hard and loved harder. The thing remembered by us will be the love she shared with all. At rest, she is with the best.

Personal Friend

12/17/11, 4/28/12 & 6/19/12

Rains come in all our lives. Trouble rumbles some days no matter what we say. Faith fades; trust goes thin, but we have a friend who attends to needs. When the devil knocks, our friend answers the door. Make it personal to grow with this friend. A personal friendship, a special kinship—my brother unlike any other. On Him you can depend.

Last Graduation

5/23/13

Thirteen years passed so very fast. Thirteen times, nine months out of each year. I now sit and wonder what is next.

We ponder what will be yonder. As time passes, we have been allowed to grow fonder of God's gifts in our lives. Family comes from near and far; they raise the bar of cheer. Family makes fear of the unknown disappear. The graduate is older but still young in so many ways. It is fair to say they are equipped to move forward with each day's grace. Equipped, we say, to run the race in the world with God's grace. Graduation is not final but a continuation toward God's final.

The Bigs

3/27/12

Not identical in any way. Twins at birth.

Both had hearts that were fully charged.

Big boy was a man who cared for all.

Blue, an essential person of plain

common wisdom.

Both workers who loved working.

Both gone to soon.

Is it true only the good die young?

They were brothers like none other.

I, for one, miss them for their down-to-earth ways. They had a unique way of holding demons at bay. They left us the better having them the short time they were with us. The bigs loved to visit family. To this day, I am the same way. The bigs' acts of love and life live on with the family. Big Blue always true. Big Boy, what a joy. Big gifts to us all. Thank you, God, for the big time we had together.

The Man at the Bus Stop

3/25/12

On the way home today, he waved once; he waved twice. In the one hand, he held a bottle. A smile a mile wide was on his face. I waved back from the seat I sat. The wave touched my heart, for I thought, *But for the grace of God, there go I.* This principle was not visited recently. I was moved this early Sunday afternoon after church. I was brought to a place of grace, thankfulness, from a waved hand. This bus stop took me back in time. It shook my memory positively to a spiritual core. It was a reminder of a score or more ago of how it used to be with me. God bless him; God blessed me. I should never forget the man at the bus stop.

Fill in the Blank

3/5/12

Jesus's ministry took place in the face of _____. Why do the people reject the _____? The reason He came was for His _____. As we grow in faith, we should feel more at _____. Often said but not always heard is God's _____. Think of lofty things, for heaven is _____. The cost to us is undying trust in _____. We touch with our hands, and they extend an idea. We get touched in our heart, for God forgave our _____. When the mark we set has been missed, _____knows we did our best. It is said when we hit rock bottom, that rock is Jesus at the _____. Some clichés are just a group words but are in truth _____to live by.

Aunt Tre

2/21/12

Buying things that are not needed but can be used. Who is that person? Doing the mostly unseen things. To some, it seems to mean nothing; to others, it means everything. A style, a flair, a certain positive air—who is this person? Advice that comes across like ice. The results for the advised: warmhearted relief and more belief in a spiritual life. Pleases but sometimes teases all who enter the room. What a booming, blooming approach to life. Thoughtful, never doubtful, all about what's best for this spiritual quest. Who is this person? Their thirst, the request for the best quiz all about our real test. Morals not quarrels come to mind—intense eyes followed by a smile from the heart. God has given this person to us. We ask why. Look them in the eye, and you know the how and why.

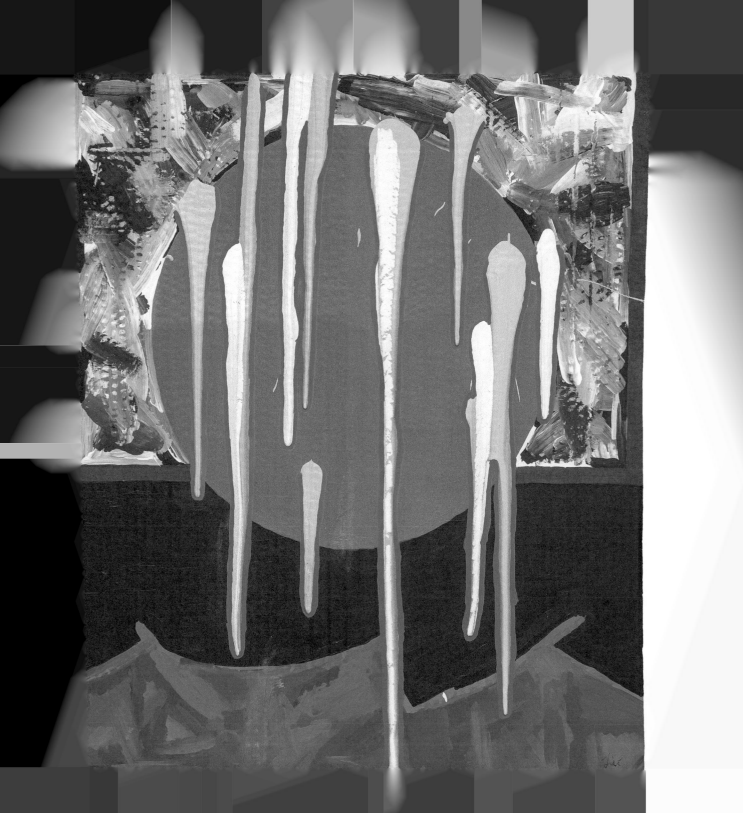

Seventeen Years Ago

11/21/11

A gift was given. A blessed event. Much joy and praise, for the miracle gave new life to view. This life is ours and yours. Ours for a short, precious time; yours for eternity. We model you and your Son for the gift given to us. A year passes quickly; each year, ever quicker it's passing. The time is near; it's clear to us all. The gift you gave to us to pass on is ready, we pray. Ready to stand every test. May faith be a large part of this life. Will our models be enough to separate from the world and always give you the best. Thank you, thank you for sharing and trusting us with your gift.

M: magnify, mindful Mariah

R: righteous, regal Rachel

W: wonder, watchful Woods

Texas

10/26/11

Home to characters beyond belief.

Home of friends whom we win.

Home of kids, their start and our blessings from God. A large place full of heart. A place that has a special place in heart, mind, and soul for all it gave and gives still. Texas can do to you what was never dreamt you could do. God is in Texas, for He is everywhere. The family of Texas is large because it is large. Boots, buckles, pickups cover the people and the roads. Old and new all at the same time. This makes it special for reasons you don't understand until you live there. Food, fellowship, brotherhood in Christ Jesus. Texas brings out the best in us.

Daughters' Friends

7/20/11

Learned a lot as the wheels turned over the highway. By the way, we listened to their thoughts about a lot. Laughter and smiles covered the miles. We left the ride. Amusement at the park as we traded one ride for another ride. Lunch in the lot, and the fun and food nourished us all. We finished with a flourish. The water tides cooled the bodies. They shared in the spirit of what's hoped for as the words poured out. The words like water refreshed all souls present like gifts from God. I pray Lord for them and us, this will always be. Your beauty of mind and soul shines bright as only your light can illuminate. Please, Lord, continue to dominate daughters' friends!

Printed in the United States
By Bookmasters